T0643921

BENCHMARK BIOGRAPHIES

Partner in Revolution
ABIGAIL ADAMS

by Clare Hodgson Meeker

BENCHMARK BOOKS

MARSHALL CAVENDISH
NEW YORK

AUTHOR'S NOTE

Because of her lack of formal schooling, Abigail never learned proper spelling and punctuation. This was something she felt self-conscious about all her life.

In order to give readers the sense of her writing, I decided to have her words printed exactly as she wrote them.

Benchmark Books
Marshall Cavendish Corporation
99 White Plains Road
Tarrytown, New York 10591-9001

© Marshall Cavendish Corporation 1998

Library of Congress Cataloging-in-Publication Data
Meeker, Clare Hodgson.
Partner in revolution : Abigail Adams / Clare Hodgson Meeker.
p.   cm. — (Benchmark biographies)
Includes bibliographical references and index.
Summary: A biography of the woman who was the wife of the second president of the United States and the mother of the sixth president.
ISBN 0-7614-0523-2 (lib. bdg.)
1. Adams, Abigail, 1744-1818—Juvenile literature. 2. Presidents' spouses—United States—Biography—Juvenile literature. 3. Adams, John, 1735-1826—Juvenile literature. [1. Adams, Abigail, 1744-1818. 2. First ladies. 3. Women—Biography. 4. Adams, John, 1735-1826.] I. Title. II. Series.
E322.1.A38L44   1988   973.4'4092   96-47790   [B]—DC21   CIP   AC

Photo research by Clare Hodgson Meeker and Dan Grausz

Photo Credits: Front cover and pages 8, 11 (top), 26, 32 (left and right), 37: U.S. Department of the Interior, National Park Service, Adams National Historic Site; back cover and pages 6, 12, 13, 14, 16, 29, 31: courtesy of the Massachusetts Historical Society; pages 11 (bottom), 21, 22, 41: © Dan Grausz; pages 18, 24, 38: courtesy, American Antiquarian Society; page 43 (left and right): National Portrait Gallery, Smithsonian Institution.

Printed in Hong Kong

1   3   5   7   8   6   4   2

CONTENTS

INTRODUCTION

When faced with a challenge what do you do? Abigail Adams lived a life that was filled with many challenges. There were times when she would despair. But, she always found a way to work things out. Abigail was so successful at this that she has earned a prominent place in history. We remember her today as a patriot on the home front during the revolutionary war years, as the wife of one United States President and the mother of another, and a woman who recorded her life for us to examine in the many letters she wrote to her family and friends.

One of Abigail's first challenges was to educate herself. Abigail pored over the books in the libraries of her father and grandfather. Eventually she acquired the knowledge to teach reading, writing, and French to her own children, including the future sixth president of the United States, John Quincy Adams. Most important, Abigail instilled in her son John Quincy the importance of service to his country.

Abigail Adams knew firsthand what service to her country meant. Often times this meant making many sacrifices. The revolutionary war years were at times very frightening and lonely for Abigail.

She became a very independent woman whom John saw as a partner who would provide support to him in overcoming many of the challenges that a life in public service would present.

As you turn each page of this wonderful history about the life of Abigail Adams, I am sure you will be impressed at how she faced so many of the challenges presented to her during her lifetime. Perhaps her successes will assist you in making your own journey through life.

Caroline Keinath
Deputy Superintendent,
Adams National Historic Site

AN INDEPENDENT SPIRIT
1744–1763

Thirteen-year-old Abigail Smith brushed a black curl out of her face, her thin lips pursed in frustration. Dipping a quill pen in the ink pot, she wrote, *"the mind is like a tender twig which you may bend as you please.* . . . (As you get older, it becomes) *like a sturdy oak, . . . hard to move."* Abigail wanted her cousin Isaac to know how lucky he was to be able to go to school. Now, while he was young, was the best time to learn.

Abigail envied her cousin. While boys and girls could go to school to learn how to write and do simple arithmetic, only boys could continue on to Latin school to prepare for college.

Abigail had never been to school. From the time she was born in 1744 she was often sick, her parents were afraid Abigail would be exposed at school to a serious illness. Their fears were real. When Abigail was seven, eleven children died of diphtheria in one week in her town of Weymouth, Massachusetts. So

This is a watercolor of the home where Abigail Smith grew up in Weymouth, Massachusetts. It was painted by an unknown artist during the period in which Abigail lived.

Abigail, her sisters Mary and Elizabeth, and her brother William were educated at home by their parents.

Reverend William Smith, Abigail's father, was the town minister of Weymouth. The son of a successful Boston businessman, he was a gentle and easygoing man who loved to farm and to collect rare books. He taught Abigail to love books and reading. Whenever Reverend Smith invited townspeople in to borrow books from his library, Abigail would curl up on the sofa and listen to their conversations.

Abigail's mother, Elizabeth Quincy Smith, came from a prominent family in the neighboring town of Braintree, Massachusetts. While she taught her daughters to cook, sew, and run a household, she also trained them to help in their community.

The Quincy family had been leaders in Braintree since the early 1600s. Abigail's grandfather Colonel John Quincy served many times as Speaker of the Massachusetts House of Representatives. While a woman's role in public life was limited, Abigail's mother did her best to continue the Quincy tradition of public service by making daily rounds with her daughters to care for the sick and offer food to those who needed it.

Abigail loved to visit her Quincy grandparents. Grandmother Quincy was *"merry and chatty,"* so different from her stern mother. Grandfather Quincy's library was even bigger than her father's. He let Abigail read as long as she wanted.

One day, Abigail overheard Grandfather Quincy angrily talking with friends.

Abigail wrote letters to family and friends from this room in the young Adamses' first home in Braintree, Massachusetts. The desk is a reproduction of the actual desk she used. A copy of her portrait sits above.

The American colonies were being forced to pay for England's wars with other countries. This new demand threatened the colonists' freedom to govern themselves.

After that visit, Abigail began to read newspapers and ask questions about England's changed attitude toward the colonies. Abigail's mother was not pleased. Women were not supposed to discuss politics. But Grandmother Quincy praised Abigail's curiosity. "Wild colts make the best horses," she said.

When Abigail was seventeen, a young lawyer named John Adams began to visit Reverend Smith's library. He was short, barrel-chested, and spoke with a commanding voice. The son of a farmer and shoemaker in Braintree, John was hardworking and ambitious. Abigail and he had lively discussions about books and politics. John's blue eyes lit with excitement when he spoke. Abigail responded with quick wit and a confident manner, her dark eyes fixing on him approvingly.

Abigail's mother was not happy about the profession John had chosen. Practicing law was not considered respectable. But Abigail did not care. Even though John teased her, saying she had an *"unladylike habit of reading, writing and thinking,"* Abigail knew their sharp minds, deep respect, and love for each other made them a good match.

THE FLAME IS KINDLED
1764-1774

Abigail married John Adams just before her twentieth birthday. They moved into the Braintree farmhouse John had inherited from his father. While John often had to travel for work, Abigail took charge of the household and immediately planted a vegetable garden. Within the year, their daughter Abigail, nicknamed Nabby, was born.

Abigail cooked over a kitchen fireplace big enough to stand in. Having to stand so close to the flame, many women died from burns suffered when their dresses caught fire. Abigail was relieved when John had the beehive oven, originally in the back of the fireplace, rebuilt outside it.

One hot summer day in 1765, Abigail sat by the open window sewing. Nabby was asleep. Suddenly, the crunch of boots on gravel woke Nabby up. A group of British soldiers, or "redcoats," was marching down the road with guns on their shoulders and bayonets flashing.

Abigail angrily shut the window. The redcoats were supposed to be there to

The kitchen fireplace in Abigail and John's home in Braintree. It includes a beehive oven cut into a brick wall (left) and a reflector oven for roasting food.

The dairy room

A portrait of Abigail Adams painted by Benjamin Blyth in 1764. Abigail was twenty-two-years-old. Blyth described Abigail's face as "about as confident, controlled and commanding a face as a woman can have and still remain feminine."

protect the colonists. But she did not like them constantly parading through the streets with weapons drawn. Now the Stamp Act the English Parliament had just passed forced them to pay a tax for stationing more British troops in the colonies.

John wrote letters to the newspaper arguing that England had no right to tax the colonists without their consent. Many colonists agreed. They chanted "no taxation without representation" and refused to buy British goods.

The British Parliament canceled the Stamp Act. But King George III was furious at the colonists for testing his authority. He demanded that Parliament impose a new tax, this time on tea.

John was away when Abigail gave birth to their second child, John Quincy, in 1767. She liked having the neighborhood women help with the birth. But once they left, she worried about having to take care of two children and the farm by herself. Abigail missed John.

So in 1768 John moved the family to Boston to be closer to his work and to the center of political activity. Abigail loved the bustling city she had often visited as a child. In the evening, she and John invited friends to their home to discuss what to do about England.

Boston was heating up with the fever of revolution. But Abigail's growing family left her little time to participate. In 1768 a third child was born. Susanna Adams was sickly from birth. For over a year, Abigail barely left the house. She watched helplessly as her daughter grew weaker. Even their good friend

A portrait of John Adams painted by Benjamin Blyth in 1764

An engraving of the Boston Massacre by Paul Revere.
Revere is known for his famous ride to warn the people
of Lexington and Concord that the British
were on the march.

Dr. Joseph Warren could not save her. Susanna died less than two years later in February of 1770.

As Abigail walked the narrow streets of Boston tending to her family's needs, she saw people angrily waving signs outside shops selling British goods. There was a different mood in the city now, one that frightened her.

On March 5, 1770, a group of young boys demonstrating outside a store began to fight with British soldiers. A boy was shot. The citizens of Boston fought back. British troops fired into the angry crowd. By the end of the day, five colonists lay dead in what was called the Boston Massacre.

The news upset Abigail, about to give birth to another child. What if it had been one of her children who had died?

People were not just talking about revolution. Now they were dying for the cause.

When John was asked to defend the British captain who was charged with murder, Abigail feared for his life. John believed it was the colonists' duty to give the British officer a fair trial and show that the colonists did not support mob violence. But Abigail and John also believed the colonists were willing to fight for their freedom.

In December 1773 ships carrying British tea dropped anchor in Boston Harbor. *"The Tea that bainful weed is arrived . . ."* Abigail wrote to a friend, *". . . the flame is kindled."*

A town meeting was held in the Old South Church to decide whether or not to pay the tax and unload the tea. Since public meetings were closed to women, Abigail had to sit by her window to hear the decision.

That evening, inside the church, a fiery debate took place. Loyalists supporting England's position argued in favor of the tax, to keep law and order in the colonies. Patriots argued against the tax, urging colonists to resist a corrupt and unjust government.

Finally, a vote was taken. The men shouted, "Huzzah!" The tax would not be paid. They would get rid of the tea. As the men left the hall, Abigail heard them chant, "Boston Harbor a teapot tonight!"

Later that night, a group of men, known as the Sons of Liberty, crept down to the harbor and boarded the ships. Dressed like Mohawk Indians with hatchets in hand, they broke open

An artist's wood engraving version of the Boston Tea Party done during the 1800s

the tea chests and emptied them into the water.

The British Parliament reacted swiftly and severely. It passed the Boston Port Act, closing Boston Harbor to all trade. The government of Massachusetts was abolished and a military governor was sent to take over. More British troops arrived.

But the harsh punishment only made the colonists more determined to fight. Abigail supported the patriot cause. *"Did ever any Kingdom or State regain their Liberty without Blood Shed?"* she wrote.

But Abigail worried about her family's safety while living in Boston. So they moved back to Braintree in the spring of 1774.

In September 1774 John left home to attend the First Continental Congress in Philadelphia as a delegate from Massachusetts. The thirteen colonies were upset by what was happening in New England and decided to meet to discuss the situation.

Abigail now had four children and a farm to manage. Nabby, age nine, John Quincy, seven, and even Charles, now four years old, could help her with the farm. But she still had an infant son, Thomas, to care for. John's parting words helped to bolster her spirits: they were now *"partners in all the joys and sorrows of the growing revolution."*

Despite John's arguments, the Congress was not ready to declare independence from England. Abigail was disappointed when the Congress decided to do nothing more than send a letter to the English Parliament threatening to cut off trade if the colonies were not listened to. The people's *"blood boils with indignation,"* Abigail wrote John. It was time for the colonies to unite in the fight for liberty.

There were many people in England who supported the colonists' cause. This political cartoon published in London in 1777 is entitled "Poor Old England Endeavoring to Reclaim Its Wicked American Children."

INDEPENDENCE AT LAST
1775–1783

On the morning of April 19, 1775, British troops marched into Lexington and Concord to seize arms and gunpowder and to capture patriot leaders. A group of raggedly dressed minutemen were waiting for them. Someone fired what is now called the "shot heard 'round the world." The American Revolution had begun.

Abigail and John's home was located on the post road between Plymouth and Boston. From the moment the war began, Abigail opened her doors to friends and neighbors whose homes were seized by British troops. She offered food and a place to rest to tired minutemen. She even melted pewter spoons to make bullets for their guns.

One week after the battles of Lexington and Concord, John left for Philadelphia to attend the Second Continental Congress. Over the next five years, Abigail became John's eyes and ears, writing him detailed letters about the war raging in Massachusetts. *Our House has been . . . the Scene of confusion. . . .*

Soldiers comeing in for lodging. . . . Refugees from Boston tierd and fatigued. . . . You can hardly imagine how we live." John read her letters to the Congress to convince them that an army should be formed to fight the redcoats.

Abigail listened while John Quincy and Nabby read the newspaper out loud. Eight-year-old John Quincy wrote his father, *"I have been trying . . . to learn to write you a letter . . . Sir. Mamma says you will accept my endeavors."*

Having never been to school, Abigail was not sure she could be a good teacher. When their husbands left to fight, women had to take on this role. Abigail taught her children with all the care she had learned from her family. She even had them read about ancient wars in other countries to help them understand the reasons for the war going on around them.

Abigail kept her family fed and clothed. Their farm provided all the food for the table. But Abigail asked John to send pins for sewing. Pins were as scarce as food.

As danger loomed closer, Abigail wrote, *"Perhaps the very next letter . . . will inform you that I am driven away from our yet quiet cottage. . . . Courage I know we have in abundance . . . but powder—where shall we get a sufficient supply?"*

On the evening of June 16, 1775, just outside the city of Charlestown (near Boston), a parade of lantern light wove silently up Bunker Hill and on to Breed's Hill. All night 500 men dug walls of earth, 6 feet high and 140 feet long, preparing to defend the city. The next morning, British generals sent ten thousand redcoats marching up Breed's Hill to fight them.

Abigail woke to the sound of distant cannon fire. It continued into the afternoon. Climbing Penn's Hill with John Quincy and Nabby, Abigail saw the entire city of Charlestown in flames.

Tears streamed down Abigail's face. How many friends and patriots died in this terrible battle? *"My bursting Heart must find vent at my pen, . . ."* Abigail later wrote John. *"Our dear Friend Dr. Warren . . . , fell gloriously fighting for his country. . . ."*

The Bunker Hill Monument as it appears today across the river from downtown Boston. This monument was built during the mid-1800s around the same time as the Washington Monument was built in Washington, D.C.

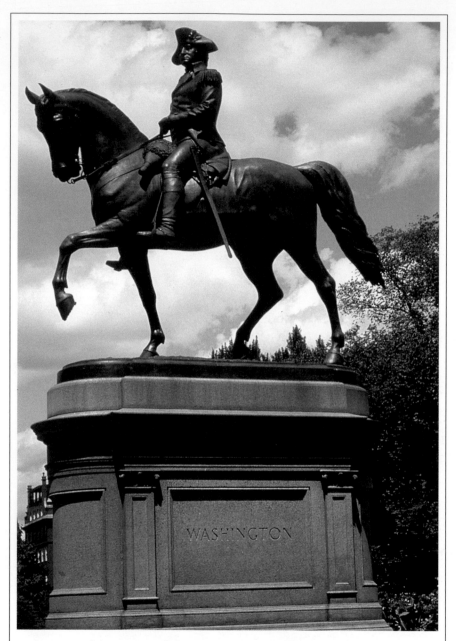

This statue of George Washington stands in the middle of the Boston Gardens in Boston.

The British won the Battle of Bunker Hill, but at great cost: 1,000 redcoats died as compared to 115 colonists. By obeying the order of their commander not to shoot "'til you see the whites of their eyes," the colonists proved they could stand bravely and fight.

Abigail's letters helped John convince the Congress to form an army under the command of George Washington. When General Washington arrived in Boston in July 1775, he brought Abigail greetings from John. At first, Abigail did not want to meet him; she did not approve of someone who owned slaves. But after his visit, she wrote John favorably about Washington: *"the Gentleman and Soldier look agreably blended in him. . . . Modesty marks every line and feature of his face."* She knew he would make a great leader.

Within a year, Washington's army forced British troops to leave Boston. Abigail began to dream of the future. If the colonies separated from Britain, a new government with new laws would have to be formed. Knowing that the Congress would be making these laws, Abigail sat down to write John her thoughts:

"Remember the Ladies, and be more generous and favorable to them than your ancestors. . . . Do not put such unlimited power into the hands of the Husbands. . . . Remember all Men would be tyrants if they could."

Under English law, women had no rights. Even though Abigail was now responsible for managing the family farm, she could not vote or own property. The educational system ignored women. When a woman married, the law gave the husband complete control over her and everything she owned.

In the new code of laws, Abigail wanted women recognized for the important role they played in the fight for independence. They needed an education. *"If we mean to have Heroes, Statesman and Philosophers,"* she wrote, *"we should have learned women."*

Abigail also wanted laws to abolish slavery. But she knew the southern colonies would object. Would people who kept slaves care enough about freedom, she wondered, to stand and fight for this new nation?

But Abigail had little time to dream of the future. A smallpox epidemic, spread by poor sanitary conditions in the military camps, hit New England. A new vaccine was available in Boston. Abigail had no time to get John's advice. She

An engraving of the public reading of the Declaration of Independence from the period.

had to act quickly.

As she watched the doctor put drops of infected pus into each child's arm, Abigail prayed that none of her children would die of the disease. Everyone survived. But Nabby's face was left permanently scarred.

Abigail and her children were still quarantined in Boston on July 4, 1776, when the Declaration of Independence was signed declaring the American colonies free from British rule. As bells clanged and cannons fired, Abigail quietly wrote John how proud she was that he *was a principal actor in laying the foundation for* (the country's) *future Greatness."*

History would remember John's leading role in creating a new nation as his greatest achievement. But at that time,

John and the other fifty-five signers of the Declaration of Independence were considered criminals under English law. Abigail feared John would be arrested at any moment.

The war for independence continued. British troops attacked New York. General Washington's army was becoming desperately short of food, clothing, and men. Winter was coming.

But by early January 1777, Washington and his troops had won several decisive battles against the British. The French, longtime enemies of England, joined the fight on the patriot side, offering money and weapons, and later, fighting troops.

In November 1777, Abigail welcomed John home. But almost as soon as he returned, he was asked to join Benjamin Franklin as an ambassador to France.

Abigail could not bear the thought of John leaving again, having to cross a dangerous ocean with enemy ships waiting to capture him. She and John had been separated for over half their married life. Hadn't they sacrificed enough for their country?

But John's heart was set on going. The struggling new nation needed the recognition and financial support of European countries. Until then, John felt his work was not complete. So Abigail, once again, had to let him go.

Abigail knew she could run the farm successfully without John. But her two older sons needed their father's attention. Abigail agreed to send eleven-year-old John Quincy, and later, ten-year-old Charles, to Europe with their father. Knowing that John would give them the best education possible comforted her.

Over the next four years, Abigail rented the farm and invested the money in other property. She became a sharp businesswoman, trading fashionable items John sent her from Europe—ribbons, fans, and lace—for things she needed at home. She kept only a few frills for herself. One was a green umbrella.

The gold locket John gave to Abigail before he sailed for Europe. The picture contains the words, "I yield Whatever is is right." Perhaps this summed up both Abigail and John's thoughts on the personal sacrifices they had made for their country.

AMERICANS ABROAD
1784-1796

In 1783, Britain signed a treaty recognizing America's independence. Thomas Jefferson sailed to Europe to help John set up trade with other countries. John asked Abigail to join him in Europe.

After nearly four years apart, Abigail was eager to see her husband and son again. But she did not look forward to the trip. Charles, now fourteen, had returned from Europe just the year before on a harrowing voyage that took three extra months. But Abigail's sisters offered to care for Charles and his twelve-year-old brother Thomas. Abigail and Nabby set sail in the summer of 1784, accompanied by two servants and a milking cow.

Their ship, called the *Active*, lived up to its name. The small ship ran into a storm off the coast of Newfoundland. Abigail and Nabby became seasick. For sixteen days they lay in their cabins while the ship battled driving rains and huge ocean swells.

When the storm ended, Abigail helped

the cook make pudding for the passengers. But the poor milking cow, badly battered by the storm, was *consigned to a watery grave,"* wrote Abigail.

Four weeks later, they landed in England and had a joyful reunion with John and John Quincy. The next day, they set out together for Paris.

John had rented a large house outside Paris with acres of formal gardens. After living in a saltbox all her life, this house was like a palace to Abigail.

Europe introduced Abigail to a whole new culture. Mozart was performing for European audiences. She heard Handel's "Hallelujah" chorus with a full orchestra, and at the ballet was shocked to see dancers show their legs.

But for Abigail, the best part of her stay in Paris was making friends with Thomas Jefferson. They had much in common. Jefferson loved books and quiet family life. They both felt strongly about education and hated slavery. Jefferson was a great admirer of the arts and often accompanied Abigail on cultural outings. Abigail wrote to her sister, *"Mr. Jefferson . . . is one of the choice ones of the earth."*

In 1785, John became ambassador to the Court of St. James and the family moved to London. Abigail had to take lessons in proper court etiquette. On the day she was to meet King George III, Abigail spent the morning dressing in her white silk gown with feathers in her hair. She spent the afternoon waiting in line. By the time the king greeted her, Abigail was too tired to say anything.

Abigail resented the stiff formality

surrounding royalty. She now under-stood why her ancestors left England for America.

Abigail began to miss home. In 1787, while briefly taking care of Jefferson's eight-year-old daughter Polly after her arrival in London from America, Abigail and John felt the joy of being with young children again. John Quincy, now 20, had returned to America. Nabby, now 22, was married to Colonel William Smith, who had served under George Washington and was John's secretary in London. Charles and Thomas soon would be grown.

So in 1788, after John had gained recognition and money from the Nether-lands for America, but had failed to persuade King George III to even discuss trade, Abigail and John returned home.

An engraving of Thomas Jefferson, whom Abigail described as "one of the choice ones of the earth."

When John and Abigail sailed into Boston Harbor, firecrackers and cannon fire welcomed them as New England's celebrated citizens. The Constitution of 1789 created a new government. George Washington was chosen as America's first president and John Adams as his vice president.

Abigail and John had only been home a few months when the news came. John left for New York to be sworn in. Abigail, thrilled at being reunited with her family again, promised to follow once she had gotten their new home in order.

During the years John was away in Europe, Abigail had purchased a larger home with money she had carefully saved. As she planted lilacs and the rose bushes she had brought from England at her new home, Abigail felt a sense of pride. Her husband was now vice president. Even though his salary was small, Abigail felt confident that she could make money from the acres of fruit trees on her new property.

A year later, Abigail joined John in New York, the nation's first capital. He had rented a house in Richmond Hill. Nabby lived nearby with her husband and children. Abigail's three sons were at Harvard now, but she insisted that Charles accompany her to New York. He was drinking too much and socializing with the wrong people at school. Abigail did not want Charles to end up like her brother William, who had died an alcoholic at age forty-one.

Abigail's duties as wife of the vice president left little time for family. She

A color engraving of the Boston Statehouse from the period.

*A portrait of Nabby, Abigail Adams 2nd, dressed in the fashionable European style
and a portrait of her brother Charles Adams, in miniature.*

admired Martha Washington who greeted guests *"with great ease and politeness."* But the social demands were exhausting.

When the nation's capital changed to Philadelphia, Abigail and John moved again. Their son Thomas came down with a terrible fever while visiting them. For two weeks Abigail stumbled over packing boxes, shuttling between Thomas's bedroom and the living room to greet visitors.

Thomas recovered. But then Abigail became very sick. She returned to Braintree where her sisters and friends took care of her.

Abigail's health slowly improved. In 1792, Braintree was renamed the town of Quincy in honor of Abigail's grandfather, John Quincy. Abigail took a renewed interest in her community, though she didn't always agree with her neighbors' opinions. A young black boy who worked for Abigail could not go to school, because the neighbors would not let him attend with their children. So Abigail taught him in her own home.

In 1792, John began his second term as vice president. France asked for America's help with its own revolution. But President Washington wanted America to remain neutral in any wars in Europe.

Many Americans disagreed, comparing the French Revolution to their own fight for liberty. Thomas Jefferson, while he was still in France, had supported the French peasants early in the revolution. Believing the spirit of resistance should always be kept alive, Jefferson, now secretary of state, disagreed with the president.

The French Revolution grew more and more violent. Abigail was horrified when King Louis XVI and his wife, Marie Antoinette, were beheaded in 1793.

Remembering Boston's angry mobs that roamed the streets during America's revolution, Abigail and John agreed with President Washington. *"An unprincipled mob is the worst of all Tyrannies,"* Abigail wrote.

Weary of the fighting within his own government, Washington announced he would retire from the presidency in 1796. Abigail wrote to John, *"All America ought to be in mourning. . . . We shall not look upon his like again."*

WASHINGTON AND PEACEFIELD
1797–1818

Congress was divided into two political parties: the Republicans, headed by Thomas Jefferson, and the Federalists, who supported John Adams. For the first time, there was a race for the presidency.

Neither Thomas Jefferson nor John Adams actively campaigned. They thought it was undignified. The Constitution decreed that the person who received the most votes would be president. The runner-up would be vice president. John Adams won by three votes.

Abigail's poor health prevented her from attending John's presidential inauguration on March 4, 1797. As she gazed out the window at the small, green shoots pushing up in her garden, Abigail thought of her family. John Quincy was now minister to the Netherlands. Thomas had accompanied him as his secretary. Nabby and Charles, both married with children, lived with their families in New York. Like tender shoots, they were making their way in the world. She hoped they would grow to be strong.

When spring arrived, Abigail traveled by coach to Philadelphia. *"I must impose a silence upon myself when I long to talk,"* she wrote John, knowing that as first lady, she would have to watch what she said in public. But in private, she was still John's most trusted advisor.

Abigail's days were filled with receiving visitors and planning menus for fancy dinners with members of Congress and foreign dignitaries. In a letter to her sister, Abigail called it *"splendid misery."*

John faced his first crisis as president when French ships began attacking American vessels. Believing the country was not ready for war, John strengthened the navy and launched the *USS Constitution* to help fend off attacks by French ships. He also asked Washington to take command of the army again.

Eventually, the French backed down.

For a brief time, Abigail's husband was a hero. But the press criticized him when John Quincy was appointed minister to Prussia. Abigail thought these attacks by the press were *"criminal."* She and John believed there should be some restraints to keep reporting truthful and decent.

In 1798, John signed into law the Alien and Sedition Acts, which made it a crime to criticize the government, the president, or Congress. This law made John extremely unpopular. Having drafted the Bill of Rights to protect the people against unfair acts of government, Thomas Jefferson called it a violation of the Constitution.

John and Abigail's children were also in trouble. Nabby's husband had no steady job and abandoned his family for months at a time. Charles was drinking heavily and his health was suffering. John Quincy had recently married an American girl who had grown up in Europe. Abigail feared that Louisa Catherine was too used to the fashionable life to be happy in America.

But hearing John comment that George Washington was lucky to be childless, Abigail firmly replied, *"If he has none to give him pain, he has none to give him pleasure."*

On December 14, 1799, George Washington died. For a brief time, people forgot their political differences and came together to mourn. But by spring, Jefferson's party was gaining popularity by opposing the Alien and Sedition Acts.

Late in 1800, John and Abigail moved into the White House in Washington, the new capital. The huge mansion was unfinished, with no furniture or running water. Abigail lit fires in all thirteen fireplaces to keep out the cold. She used the

This is Abigail's rose china with cow handles which she had made for her in Europe. This china is on display at the Adams Historical Site.

This is an early drawing of the White House as it looked when John and Abigail lived there. It was George Washington's vision that the president should live in a stately home. Washington hired the architect who designed the White House, but it was not completed until after his presidency. Abigail and John became its first inhabitants.

large, empty rooms for hanging wash. Neither Abigail nor John were happy living there.

But when John was defeated by Thomas Jefferson in the presidential election of 1800, Abigail was sorry to leave. She was sad that people did not support her husband after he had given so much to his country. To add to their grief, their son Charles, who had never stopped drinking, died at age 30, the same day Jefferson was elected.

A cold winter still gripped the nation in the weeks before Jefferson's inauguration. John was still president. Abigail decided to make the dangerous journey home by herself. As her carriage rolled past stark, white wilderness and frozen rivers, fifty-seven-year-old Abigail tried to forget the pain of the last few months and look forward to returning to Quincy for good.

Still bitter over his defeat, John refused to attend Jefferson's presidential inauguration. Their friendship was now severely strained. John chose instead to set off for Quincy in the early hours of that day.

Abigail and John threw themselves into their new life. John called their new house "Peacefield" for the peace of mind it gave him. Abigail wrote Nabby that she was now a *dairywoman . . .* (up) *at five o'clock in the morning skimming my milk.*"

In 1801, John Quincy returned home from Europe with his wife, Louisa Catherine, and son. It had been six years since Abigail and John had seen them. In 1803, John Quincy became a senator from Massachusetts. He later was appointed secretary of state, well on his way to becoming the nation's sixth president.

But Abigail still mothered him. *"I wish you would not let him go to Congress without a cracker in his jacket,"* she wrote his wife. It was hard to stand your ground, Louisa Catherine admitted, with a mother-in-law who was *"the guiding planet around which all revolved."*

Thomas married and settled in Quincy, becoming a judge. Nabby and her children often visited. Abigail loved cooking large dinners for her family and watching John play with his grandchildren.

In 1804, Abigail learned that Thomas Jefferson's daughter Polly had died in childbirth. She and Jefferson had not spoken in years. But her vivid memory of taking care of Polly in Europe and her

grief over Charles's death forced Abigail to break her silence and comfort an old friend. *"The powerful feelings of my heart,"* she wrote Jefferson, *"have . . . called upon me to shed the tear of sorrow."*

President Jefferson soon wrote back, attempting to renew their friendship and discuss their political differences. After several letters back and forth that Abigail kept secret from John, she ended the correspondence. But Abigail had paved the way for the two men to renew their friendship eight years later.

In 1811, Nabby was diagnosed with breast cancer. The surgery was performed at Peacefield, so Abigail could take care of her daughter. The operation to remove the cancer was short but very dangerous, with no anesthetic to numb the pain.

Peacefield as it looks today. John named it in honor of the peace he had worked on so hard to achieve for his country and for the peace of mind the house gave him and Abigail.

At first, the operation appeared to be successful. Nabby returned to New York. But a year later, the cancer was back. At age 48, Nabby returned to Quincy to die in her parents' home. Her daughter Caroline continued to live with Abigail and John until she married. Writing to John Quincy of his sister's death, Abigail cried, *"I have lost, O what have I not lost in . . . my only daughter."*

In 1818, Abigail Adams developed typhoid fever and was confined to bed. She died just before her 74th birthday.

"The dear Partner of my Life for fifty-four Years" is gone, John wrote to Thomas Jefferson. Abigail would have been happy to know that her two lifelong patriots remained friends until their deaths on the same day, July 4, 1826, fifty years after the signing of the Declaration of Independence.

Abigail once wrote from her bedroom window at Peacefield, *"the Beauties which my garden unfolds . . . tempt me to forget the past."* Abigail had endured much sadness in her life, outliving three of her children, her brother, and her two sisters. But Abigail's deep commitment to her country's independence and her lasting love for John forged a partnership that helped create a new nation and guide it peacefully in its early years.

These silhouettes of Abigail and John were a popular style of portrait during their lifetime.
These were executed by Raphaelle Peale in 1809. Abigail was 65 years old, and John was 74.

Glossary

Anesthetic: Any drug that causes a numbing sensation.

Bayonet: A daggerlike steel weapon that is attached to the muzzle of a rifle.

Bee-Hive Oven: A brick-lined hole in the back of a fireplace used for baking.

Minutemen: Members of America's fighting forces before and during the Revolutionary War.

Pewter: A combination of tin and lead used for utensils and serving vessels.

Post Road: Main road used for carrying the mail.

Quarantined: A strict isolation imposed to prevent the spread of disease.

Redcoats: A name for British soldiers based on the color of the uniforms they wore.

Saltbox: A house with a steeply pitched roof built mainly in New England in colonial times.

To Learn More About Abigail Adams

* This book includes quotations from letters of Abigail Adams and her family. These letters can be found in the Adams Papers, the collection of family manuscripts located at the Massachusetts Historical Society.

Another source of these letters is L. H. Butterfield's *The Book of Abigail and John: Selected letters of the Adams Family 1762–1784,* published by the Massachusetts Historical Society, 1975.

Bober, Natalie S. *Abigail Adams: Witness to a Revolution.* New York: Atheneum, 1995.

Brenner, Barbara. *If You Were There in 1776.* New York: Simon & Schuster, 1994.

Fritz, Jean. *Can't You Make Them Behave, King George.* New York: Coward McCann, 1977.

Gibbons, Gail. *From Path to Highway: The Story of the Boston Post Road.* New York: T. Y. Crowell, 1986.

Gregory, Kristina. *The Winter of Red Snow: The Revolutionary War Diary of Abigail Jane Stewart*. New York: Scholastic, 1996.

Hakim, Joy. *From Colonies to Country*. New York: Oxford University Press, 1993.

Mayo, Edith P. *The Smithsonian Book of First Ladies*. New York: Henry Holt, 1996.

Meltzer, Milton. *The American Revolutionaries: A History in Their Own Words (1750–1800)*. New York: HarperCollins, 1987.

Murphy, Jim. *A Young Patriot: The American Revolution as Experienced By One Boy*. New York: Clarion Books, 1996.

Index

Page numbers for illustrations are in boldface

ABOUT THE AUTHOR

Clare Hodgson Meeker was born and raised in the New York City area. She graduated with a B.A. degree in music from Boston University and received a law degree from Hofstra University. Her love of research and of reading books with her children led her to begin her career as a children's writer. Her previous books include *A Tale of Two Rice Birds*, an adaptation of a folktale from Thailand, and *Who Wakes Rooster?* which won the Pacific Northwest Writers Conference Picture Book Award in 1993. She also composes music for and sings with a group called "The Righteous Mothers." Clare Meeker lives with her husband and two children in Mercer Island, Washington.